JAMAICA
WORLD ADVENTURES
BY STEFFI CAVELL-CLARKE

BookLife

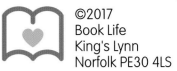

©2017
Book Life
King's Lynn
Norfolk PE30 4LS

ISBN: 978-1-78637-033-4

All rights reserved
Printed in Malaysia

Written by:
Steffi Cavell-Clarke

Edited by:
Grace Jones

Designed by:
Drue Rintoul

A catalogue record for this book
is available from the British Library.

JAMAICA
WORLD ADVENTURES

CONTENTS

Words in **red** can be found in the glossary on page 24.

WHERE IS JAMAICA?

Jamaica is an island in the Caribbean Sea.
The capital city of Jamaica is Kingston.

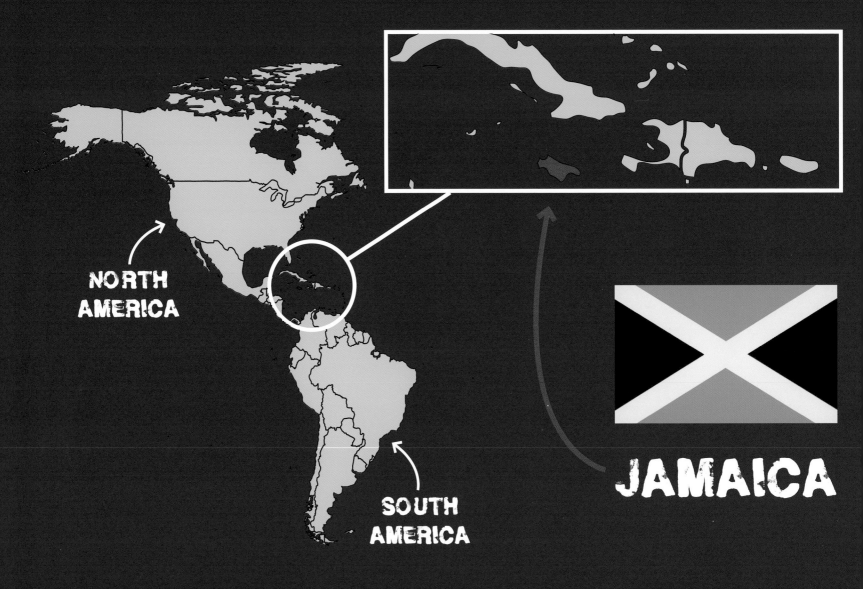

NORTH AMERICA

SOUTH AMERICA

JAMAICA

The **population** of Jamaica is over two and a half million. Lots of **tourists** visit Jamaica for the hot weather and to spend time at the beach.

WEATHER AND LANDSCAPE

Jamaica has a **tropical climate**. It is mostly hot and sunny all year round. The hottest months of the year are July and August.

Jamaica has lots of tropical rainforests, high mountains and many waterfalls. The largest waterfall in Jamaica is Dunn's River Falls.

DUNN'S
RIVER FALLS, JAMAICA

CLOTHING

Children in Jamaica mostly wear cool and comfortable clothing because of the hot weather.

Many Jamaican women wear traditional headscarves. They are made out of soft, colourful cotton and are wrapped around the head.

HEADSCARF

RELIGION

The most popular religion in Jamaica is Christianity. A Christian place of worship is a church. Christians usually go to church every Sunday for prayer.

Christians can also go to church to worship God and read from the Christian holy book, known as the Bible.

INSIDE A CHURCH

FOOD

Jerk is a traditional style of cooking in Jamaica. This is when meat is cooked with hot spices over a small fire.

JERK CHICKEN

Ackee is the **national** fruit of Jamaica. It is often cooked with salty fish and served for breakfast.

ACKEE FRUIT

AT SCHOOL

Children in Jamaica start school at the age of six.
They go to school to learn how to read and write.

Children often learn how to play sports at school, such as athletics, football and cricket.

AT HOME

COFFEE BEAN

Some people in Jamaica live in small villages or on farms. They often grow crops, such as coffee beans.

Most people in Jamaica live in big cities and towns, such as Kingston and Falmouth.

FALMOUTH

KINGSTON

CARIBBEAN SEA

Montego Bay
Falmouth
Discovery Bay
Saint Ann's Bay
Duncans
Runaway Bay
Oracabessa
Brown's Town
Ocho Rios
Port Maria
Moneague
Montpelier
Annotto Bay
Buff Bay

JAMAICA

Christiana
Linstead
Frankfield
Black River
Mandeville
May Pen
Old Harbour
Spanish Town
Half Way Tree
KINGSTON
Portmore
Bull Bay
Alligator Pond
The Alley
Port Esquivel
Portland Bight
Morant Bay
Long Bay

CARIBBEAN SEA

FAMILIES

Many children in Jamaica live with their parents and **siblings**. Lots of families like to live close to their grandparents, aunts and uncles.

Jamaican families like to get together to celebrate special occasions like weddings.

SPORT

One of the most popular sports in Jamaica is athletics. This includes running, jumping and throwing competitions.

The Jamaican **athlete** Usain Bolt is believed to be the fastest runner in the world. He has won six Olympic gold medals and may win many more.

FUN FACTS

Reggae music was created in Jamaica and has become a very popular type of music all around the world.

The largest butterfly in Jamaica is called the giant swallowtail. Its wings are over 14 centimetres wide.

GLOSSARY

athlete	someone who is skilled at sport
island	an area of land that is surrounded by water
national	common to a country
population	amount of people living in that place
siblings	brothers and sisters
tourists	visitors from other countries
traditional	ways of behaving that have been done for a long time
tropical climate	warm and wet weather

INDEX

Photocredits: Abbreviations: l-left, r-right, b-bottom, t-top, c-centre, m-middle.

Front Cover, 3, 12, 15 – diogoppr. 1 – Aleksey Klints. 2, 11 – Ksenia Ragozina. 4inset – Globe Turner. 4 – chrupka. 5, 9, 16 – Filipe Frazao. 6 – Jefferson Bernardes. 7t – earlytwenties. 7inset – Xico Putini. 7b – ostill. 8, 24 – Samuel Borges Photography. 8 – Paulo Nabas. 13, 18, 19inset – Monkey Business Images. 14 – michaeljung. 16inset – Wilson Araujo. 17 – Olena Bloshchynska. 19 – Spotmatik Ltd. 20 – MarcusVDT. 20inset – Beto Chagas. 21 – Will Rodrigues. 21inset – Digital Storm. 22 – Olga_i. 22tr – Heiko Kiera. 22bl – Erni. 23t – moomsabuy. 23b – Christian Vinces. 24 – Zurijeta. Images are courtesy of Shutterstock.com. With thanks to Getty Images, Thinkstock Photo and iStockphoto.